D1361324

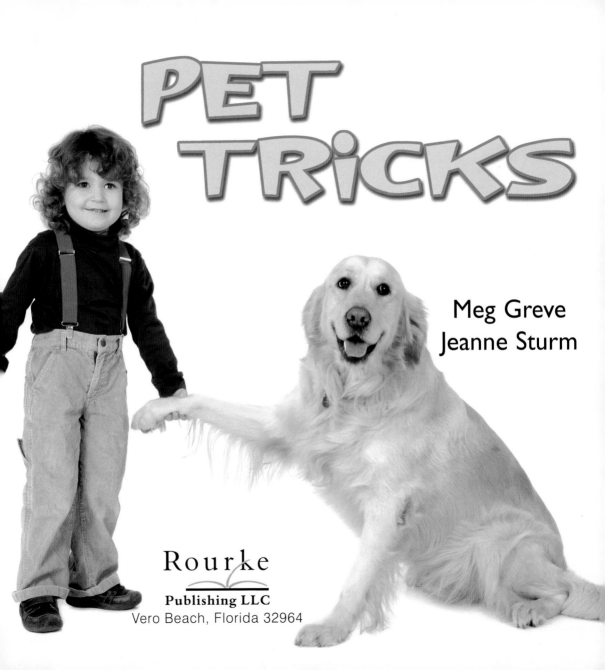

PET TRICKS

Meg Greve
Jeanne Sturm

Rourke
Publishing LLC
Vero Beach, Florida 32964

www.rourkepublishing.com

PHOTO CREDITS: © Eric Isselée: Cover, page 4, 10, 16; © Dragan Trifunovic: Title Page; © Eline Spek: page 3 left; © Boris Katsman: page 3 bottom right; © Andraz Cerar: page 3 top right; © Jill Lange: page 5; © Erik Lam: page 6; © Frédéric De Bailliencourt: page 7; © Serdar Yagci: page 8; © Dainis Derics: page 9; © Juergan Bosse: page 11; © Maria Bibikova: page 12; © Dusan Zidar: page 13; © Heinrich Volschenk: page 14; © Sebastian Duda: page 15; © Emmanuelle Bonzami: page 17, 20 right; © Oleg Kozlov: page 18, 19; © Eileen Hart: page 20 left; © Shelly Perry: page 21 bottom left; © Miroslava Arnaudova: page 21 top right;

Editor: Kelli Hicks

Cover design by: Nicola Stratford: bdpublishing.com

Interior design by: Renee Brady

Library of Congress Cataloging-in-Publication Data

Greve, Meg.
  Pet tricks / Meg Greve, Jeanne Sturm.
    p. cm. -- (My first discovery library)
  ISBN 978-1-60472-530-8
  1. Pets--Juvenile literature. I. Sturm, Jeanne. II. Title.
  SF416.2G77 2009b
  636.088'7--dc22
                          2008025167

Printed in the USA

CG/CG

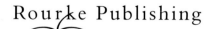

www.rourkepublishing.com – rourke@rourkepublishing.com
Post Office Box 3328, Vero Beach, FL 32964

Pets can do
amazing things.

3

My **parrot**
flaps and
flies in
his cage.

Flap, flap, flap.

My dog loves to
run and play
catch on
the beach.

Run, run, run.

6

My **iguana** creeps and lies on it's branch.

Creep, creep, creep.

My **ferret** sneaks through the garden.

Sneak, sneak, sneak

11

My **kitten** loves to
crawl through
the grass.

Crawl, crawl, crawl.

My **chameleon** changes color when he is cold.

Change, change, change.

15

My **horse** and I jump over a fence.

Jump, jump, jump.

17

My pet rat
climbs up
my shirt.

Climb, climb, climb.

What kind of tricks can your pet do?

21

Glossary

chameleon (kuh-MEE-lee-uhn): A chameleon is a lizard that can change its color. Chameleons can make many different patterns and colors. Sometimes chameleons change color to attract a mate.

ferret (FER-it): A ferret is a long, thin animal in the weasel family. Ferrets enjoy carrying things off to secret hiding places. Ferrets are most active at dusk and dawn.

kitten (KIT-uhn): A kitten is a baby cat. A kitten does not open its eyes for seven to ten days after its birth. The mother cat's milk is important to help the kitten grow strong and healthy.

horse (HORSS): A horse is a mammal with a long neck, long legs, a mane, and a tail. People ride horses, or use them to carry loads and pull heavy objects.

iguana (i-GWAN-uh): An iguana is a large lizard. Iguanas eat plants. Iguanas can grow to more than five feet long.

parrot (PA-ruht): A parrot is a tropical bird with brightly colored feathers. Many parrots can learn to repeat words and sounds. Parrots enjoy eating seeds, fruits, and nectar.

Index

Further Reading

Meadows, Daisy. *Harriet the Hamster Fairy*. Orchard Books, 2008.

Selig, Josh. *Good Night, Wonder Pets!* Little Airplane Productions, 2008

Dodd, Emma. *What Pet to Get?* Scholastic, 2008.

Websites

http://www.kidzworld.com/article/1740-colors-of-a-chameleon

http://animals.howstuffworks.com/animal-facts/animal-camouflage2.htm

http://animals.howstuffworks.com/mammals/horse-info.htm

About the Authors

Meg Greve, an elementary teacher, lives in Chicago with her family. Currently, she is taking some time to enjoy being a mother and reading to her own children every day.

Jeanne Sturm and her family live in Florida, along with one dog, two rabbits, and many fish. Astro, the family dog, knows a few tricks, and is in the process of learning even more.